THIS BOOK

BELONGS TO

....

....

Thank you for Purchasing my book and taking the time to read it from front to back. I am always grateful when a reader chooses my work and I hope you enjoyed it!

With the vast selection available online, I am touched that you chose to be purchasing my work and take valuable time out of your life to read it. My hope is that you feel you made the right decision.

I very much would like to know what you thought of the book. Please take the time to write an honest and informative review on Amazon.com. Your experience and opinions will be of great benefit to me and those readers looking to make an informed choice.

With much thanks.

@COPYRIGHT 2024

Table of Contents

This Book Is for You: 5

Why This Book Is Different from Other Weight Loss books: 6

What You Will Gain from This Book: 7

What Is Autosuggestion? 8

How To Use This Book: 9

Important notice: 10

Chapter 1 11

Chapter 2 20

What is the Gulo? 21

Chapter 3 36

Chapter 4 45

Chapter 5 55

Summary 67

Some Key Points to Remember: 68

Be aware of the Gulo 70

THIS BOOK IS FOR YOU:

◇ If you want to break the cycle of diet, weight loss, and regaining all the lost weight.

◇ If you want to stop being frustrated over food that you are not allowed to eat, even though you want to.

◇ If you want to learn to eat based on your physical needs, such as real hunger, and not because you're controlled by emotional needs and impulses.

WHY THIS BOOK IS DIFFERENT FROM OTHER WEIGHT LOSS BOOKS:

◇ This book is based on an autosuggestion technique. It doesn't present any specific diet regime or physical training program.

◇ The book suggests a different and innovative way of thinking about food and the reasons we eat.

◇ The book brings to light subconscious destructive thinking patterns about food and eating, and will guide you through a process that will replace them with helpful, constructive thinking patterns that will enable you to be thin.

◇ This short book is easy and enjoyable to read. It contains concise and precise insights, accompanied by illustrations that will help you remember them.

WHAT YOU WILL GAIN FROM THIS BOOK:

◇ You won't eat because you are sad, nervous or tense.

◇ You will stop constantly planning and thinking about what you are going to eat next. You'll think about food only when you're physically hungry.

◇ You won't feel the constant need to snack.

◇ You'll be able to tell when you're already full, and your body doesn't need to go on eating. You will be able to stop eating, even if there is more of your favorite food on your plate.

◇ When you attend an event, where special delicacies are served, you will be able to eat just a bit, to enjoy their taste, and no more than that.

◇ When you sit at a meeting where refreshments are served, you will not eat just because others are eating.

◇ You'll be content with two bites of chocolate, instead of eating the whole bar.

WHAT IS AUTOSUGGESTION?

◇ Autosuggestion is a psychological technique through which people can change their attitudes, feelings, and beliefs using self-persuasion. The process can be used in a variety of areas: career, health, relationships, and more.

◇ Autosuggestion can be used to convince the subconscious mind of positive things or to change a particular behavior. A common autosuggestion technique is to repeat positive and empowering statements until the subconscious mind accepts them as true.

◇ However, the subconscious mind can accept a new habit or insight only if it has had at least a few experiences to strengthen it.

HOW TO USE THIS BOOK:

◇ This book will change your eating habits using the power of autosuggestion. It provides the concepts and insights you'll need to change your perception of food and of eating, and advice on how to behave in different food-related situations.

◇ In order to succeed, you should:

◇ Read the book repeatedly (preferably - every day), until the concepts introduced here come to mind automatically, in all kinds of food-related situations.

◇ Repeat the first two chapters of the book to yourself all the time, even get to know them by heart.

◇ Know that even after you've internalized the new insights, you'll still have to remind yourself of them from time to time. Our brain tends to return to patterns ingrained in it since childhood.

IMPORTANT NOTICE:

◇ Sometimes overeating is caused by serious mental and health issues. If this is the case, you should consult your doctor before using this book.

◇ If you begin feeling anxious or guilty about eating, stop reading this book and consult a health care professional.

◇ If using this book makes you feel uncomfortable or stressed about the subject of eating, stop reading this book.

Chapter 1

The True Meaning of Food

●●●●●●●●●●●●●●●●●●●●●●●●●●●●●●●●●●

*Learn these messages by heart to
change your attitude towards food.*

**FOOD IS NOTHING MORE
THAN THE FUEL FOR THE BODY.**

••••••••••••••••••••••••••••••••

I do not eat in order to enjoy myself.
If I enjoy eating, that's great, but I do not eat for enjoyment.
I eat to enable my body to move, to think, to have fun, to love and more.

When I fill up my car with gas, it spills out as soon as the tank is full.

When I eat more than my body needs, the food doesn't spill out and overflow.
The body is much more sophisticated than a car, and it stores the food in the form of fat reserves. In case I need food later.

In prehistoric times this miraculous mechanism helped men and women survive harsh winters, when there was no food around.

Today, we can get something to eat at any given time. We no longer need this mechanism. In fact, it hurts us!
Fat reserves that used to protect us are unhealthy, and are also perceived as unaesthetic.

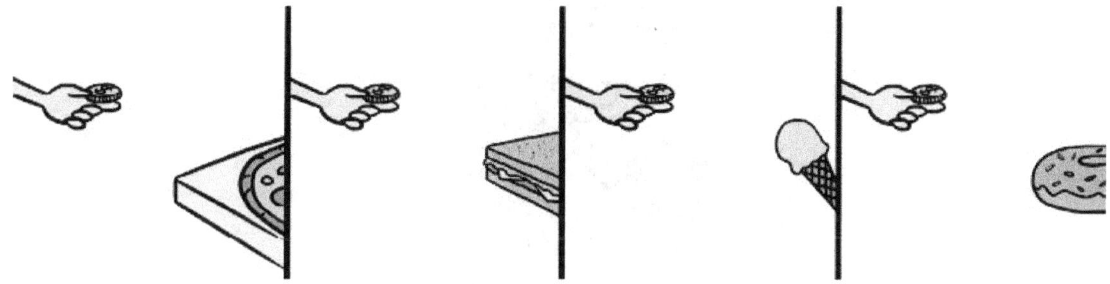

The solution seems simple: I will eat only when I'm hungry. This way I will not accumulate the body fat which I do not want, and do not need.

BUT IT'S NOT THAT SIMPLE.

●●●●●●●●●●●●●●●●●●●●●●●●●●●●●●●●●●●●●●

Chapter 2

The Gulo

••••••••••••••••••••••••••••••••••••

Learn these messages by heart in order to look differently at the need to eat, and to understand it better.

WHAT IS THE GULO?

There are all kinds of psychological and scientific theories that try to explain the causes of human behavior and feelings. At the time Freud talked about the **id** as a part of the human psyche structure that is unconscious, and causes a person to act on impulses rather than rational thinking. Nowadays it is more common to talk about the **Lizard Brain** (composed of the Reptilian brain and limbic system) as being in charge of human's impulses and instincts. However, the features of both are the same:

They are primitive and do not change with time or experience. They are not in touch with the external world. They are not affected by reality or logic. They operate only within the unconscious part of the mind.

The **id** is driven by the pleasure principle and the Lizard Brain by the reward circuit. That means they seek immediate satisfaction of every urge, regardless of the consequences. When they are denied, we experience frustration and tension.

When we try to eat only as much as we need, we are confronted with our desires. The desire to eat more, much more than what we need.

I call this desire the **"Gulo"** (Gulo is Latin for "glutton"), and it has characteristics that are similar, in my opinion, to those of the **id's** and the **Lizard Brain**.

Knowing the following sentences by heart will help you identify where the urge to eat is coming from — a real physical hunger or a very insistent Gulo....

● ●

The problem is that the Gulo is inside of me. If it were up to it, I would eat, chew and mash food in my mouth all day long, and in between drink sweetened juice.

It doesn't care if binge eating is not good for me, and it doesn't have any connection to my true desires and thoughts about overeating. It'll do anything to make me eat.

It will repeatedly place a picture of delicious food in my mind. It will make me feel hungry, even though I just ate. It will try to convince me that I need comfort in the form of food, and that eating it will make me happy.

This is how ridiculous situations are created. Say I am moody because I am single. The Gulo suggests that I eat as a consolation, as if two bites from a cake will bring Prince Charming to my door...

Or I can be upset because I've put on some weight, and my favorite dress doesn't suit me anymore. The Gulo will try to make me eat to console myself…

The Gulo makes me feel hungry even if I just ate. Even seeing someone else eating something nice can make the Gulo try to convince me to eat it as well.

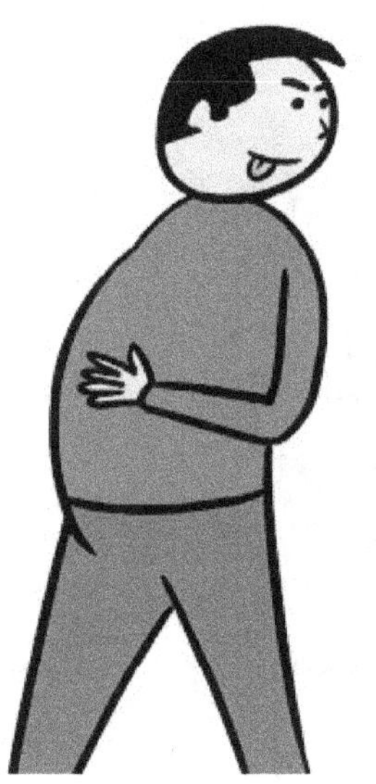

It can drive me crazy by projecting images of delicious food into my mind and repeating it again and again until I break down and eat it.

THE PURPOSE OF MEMORIZING THE FOLLOWING SENTENCES BY HEART IS TO HELP YOU THINK TWICE IF IT'S TRULY WORTH EATING WHAT YOU DESIRE SO MUCH, AND HOW MUCH DO YOU NEED TO EAT FROM IT IN ORDER TO ENJOY IT.

•••••••••••••••••••••••••••••••••

What can I do when the Gulo nags me and tries to persuade me to **chew and mash food in my mouth?**

What must I remember?

I must remember that the **first bite** tastes terrific!

There is a change in my mouth from nothing to something delicious.

My mouth fills up with a delicious sensation. Taste buds will signal the brain excitedly. I can hear the angels sing Hallelujah!

The **second bite** also tastes delicious, and I still enjoy it very much. Just not as much as the first bite, since my mouth fills up with the same food as before.

By the time I take the **third bite, or at most - the fourth,** I start to think about other things, like a dress I saw in a shop window, a conversation I had with my friend, or something my boss said to me... My brain becomes accustomed to the stimulus of food and is now looking for the next exciting thing to think about.

Suddenly the food is all gone, and I feel bad about myself and regret eating.

A few days later I might also notice I've put on some weight. All the food I ate when I wasn't really hungry is taking its toll.
I get depressed and feel uncomfortable with my body and how I look. I feel disappointed in myself, even hating myself for not looking the way I want to.

Not to mention that being overweight is not good for my health.

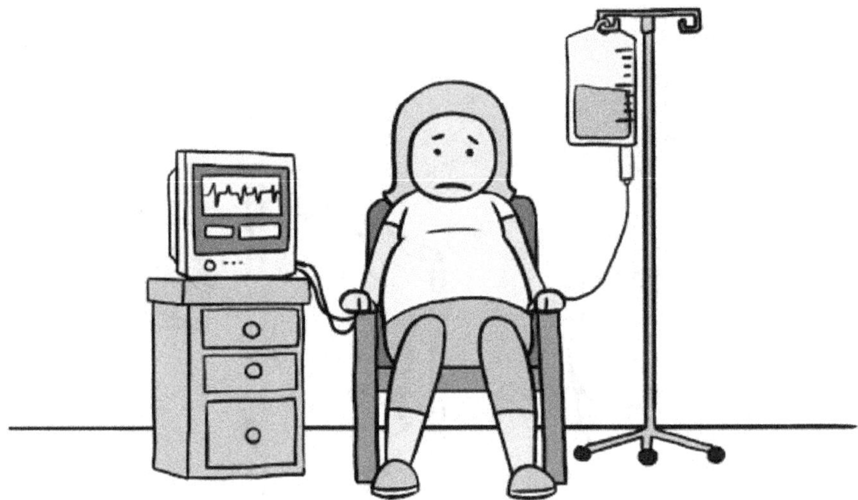

Is the minute of pleasure really worth all this misery and disappointment? After all, the joy of looking at myself in the mirror and feeling satisfied is much more profound, meaningful, and lasts much longer, than the brief pleasure of chewing and mashing food in my mouth.

Chapter 3

Fight the Gulo

There are several ways to fight your Gulo.

You can **ignore the images of food** that the Gulo projects in front of your eyes. Force yourselves to think of something else. It's not easy, but it is possible, and the more you do it, the easier it gets.

When the Gulo whispers in your ear, "Come on, eat this delicious treat, indulge yourself, you deserve it, don't be so harsh on yourself...", always remember that **indulging yourself like this is not a treat. It is, in fact, a punishment.** It leads to obesity and to feeling sad and disappointed. Those lousy feelings arrive right after you finish eating - and again a few days later, when you see that you've put on weight. **Real indulgence is feeling good with yourself** when you overcome the desire to eat, or when you do things that are good for your body and soul.

You can try to **change the image the Gulo projects to you, to the image of a different food.** If the Gulo starts nagging at you to eat the other food, it shows that there is no physical need here. It is only the Gulo trying to make you chew and mash some food no matter what.

Try to **get angry at your Gulo**. It does not care about you. It is trying to get you to do something that is not in your best interest. Every time you recognize that the need to eat is not the demand of a hungry body, but the nagging of the Gulo, you can yell at it in your imagination: "Go away! Leave me alone! I don't want to eat now!"

The good news is that every time you overcome the Gulo, you make it easier to succeed next time.

However, every time the Gulo wins, every time it manages to make you eat, it becomes twice as strong. Why?
Because it is the nature of the human mind.

But you can beat the Gulo, and when you manage to overcome it, it becomes weaker and weaker.

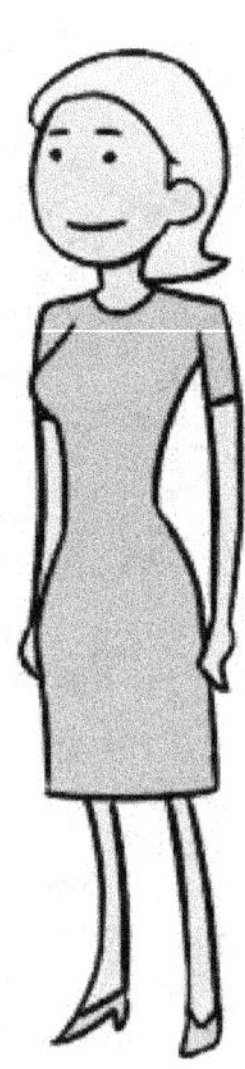

Chapter 4

Additional tools on how to manage your eating habits

•••••••••••••••••••••••••••••••••

When you eat something you like, and you don't eat it out of physical hunger, pay attention to the point where you already had the experience. When **you already understood what the taste is all about**.

What should you do at that moment?

It's simple. **Don't continue to fill your body with it**.

Look for someone to give the food to, someone who will be happy to eat it in your place, or throw it in the trash. **It's better to throw it away than to dump it into your body just because you started eating it.**

And even though it seems a shame to throw away food, **it's not as if the food you eat will pass from your belly to the stomach of a hungry child** in a third world country.

Don't say: "I should eat everything on my plate because it's a waste of money to throw food away." The money you paid for the food has already been spent. **Eating the food will not put the money back in your wallet.** At least you won't gain weight from eating it all...

Don't keep unhealthy snacks or sweets at home. Once they enter your house, the Gulo will nag you, trying to persuade you to eat them. Don't waste your efforts and energy struggling to ignore it. Avoid the situation before it has a chance to arise.

Vegetables as snacks are not a good idea. Nibbling, even vegetables, only means that you'll be constantly chewing and mashing food, regardless of hunger.

Eating like this goes against the new way of thinking you are trying to create; eating only out of actual physical hunger.

Change the way you talk about food.

Don't say: "I want to eat this." Say: **"I want to chew and mash it."** Do not say: "food." Say: **"nourishment."** The idea is to break the emotional associations of food, and to emphasize only its physical aspects.

It is essential to sever the connection between eating and pleasure, even in the way you talk about it.

The struggle with the Gulo is not just about eating. It is about every action that causes you discomfort.

Every little victory against it strengthens you. Every time you win the fight against the Gulo, it gets easier and easier to stand up to it about eating unnecessary food.

For example, when the Gulo tries to get you to use the elevator instead of climbing the stairs, or to watch television instead of cleaning the kitchen. Unfortunately, every time the Gulo wins, it becomes stronger, making it harder for you to stand up to it about eating food.

Bottom line, it is of vital importance to know how to forgive yourself! You honestly tried to restrain yourself, but in the end, you were tempted and ate what you didn't mean to eat? It's OK, don't beat yourself up. **You're human and you tried your best.** It did not go well this time. But, it will go better next time. Do not make a big deal about it!

Besides, by feeling disappointed and dissatisfied with yourself you strengthen the Gulo, too. It will use this opportunity to get you to eat more (I feel bad about myself, so I want to compensate myself by eating). **Your self-criticism damages the process.**

Chapter 5

Coping with Everyday Situations

•••••••••••••••••••••••••••••••

You're on your way home, and you feel hungry. Physical hunger, of course. It is better to **buy something and eat it now. That way you will not be hungry when you get home** and eat everything in sight.

The food you buy should be **something healthy. Whole wheat bread for example will make you feel full for a longer time.**

If you want to eat cookies, or anything that comes packaged, it is best to put some **on a plate, close the bag, and return it to the fridge or cupboard.** Sit down and eat only what you put on the plate.

That way, **you can enjoy the food and maintain control of the amount you eat.**

If you plan on enjoying a delicious snack with your coffee, it is better to cut it in half, and keep the other half for tomorrow. **Cut your half-snack into small pieces**, and eat one small piece at a time. This way, **you will enjoy the snack for longer**, and you'll feel like you've eaten the whole thing...

Make sure to always have a tasty granola snack in your bag. If you're busy running errands, or traveling from place to place, and suddenly you get hungry, it's best to have a snack on hand for when you're hungry. That way you will not be tempted to buy fattening food that you will later regret.

Sometimes you get busy. Suddenly you notice that you have not eaten for a few hours. Don't eat more than usual to compensate yourself for the lost food. On the contrary – this is an opportunity to give yourself **a gift that will help you lose more of the unwanted fat reserve**, and to look and feel better.

When visiting friends, they may serve your favorite cookies. **Take only one or two**, and that's it. There is no point in eating more. After all, **after two or three bites you will not notice that you are eating**, because you will be engrossed in the conversation about the latest news.

Besides, **you already know the taste, and you are not hungry**. Don't eat just because the cookies are there, they will only make you gain weight.

You're in the middle of running errands or shopping, and **you suddenly feel hungry**. Real physical hunger. Go ahead and buy yourself something to eat.

Just make sure **not to listen to the Gulo, who will try to get you to overeat** or choose something fattening.

Buy yourself something healthy like a small sandwich made of **whole wheat bread** for example. **It will fill you up, keep you satisfied for longer** and you will feel good about yourself.

Before you arrive at an event, a party, or any gathering that includes delicious dishes and tempting nibbles, **eat a little something**. Not something that will fill you up, but **something that will keep you from attacking the buffet**. That way you can take only what you love and in small portions. If you arrive hungry to such events, it is tough to keep yourself from munching everything in sight.

You are in a social gathering. Near the wall, there is a buffet full of some of your favorite dishes. It's hard for you to resist, even though you're not hungry. Remind yourself that **you already know what everything tastes like, and eating will not reveal anything new**. It's a shame to ingest it.
If you find it hard to get over the Gulo, **take just one item or a thin slice, only to enjoy the taste**. Do not forget that after two or three bites your enjoyment will diminish greatly. You'll hardly notice that you're eating, since you'll be busy with what's happening at the event.

You're at an event, and unfortunately, you're hungry. There's a buffet with lots of delicious and unique delicacies you do not get to eat every day.

Go ahead and enjoy yourself. Just keep in mind that **you do not have to load up your plate. You can have just a little bit of everything.**

You can even forgo the bread. After all, you know what it tastes like. Focus on the tasty and nutritious delights you don't normally enjoy.

And if you taste something and don't like it, stop. **It's a shame to continue eating something just because it is on your plate**. Make sure to set the plate down on the first table you see (don't continue holding the plate - you'll just eat from it without even noticing).

Summary

SOME KEY POINTS TO REMEMBER:

◇ Food is only fuel for the body. You do not eat to enjoy yourself. If you enjoy eating that's great, but you do not eat for enjoyment. You eat to feed your body.

◇ Start eating only when you're hungry, and stop eating as soon as you realize you're not hungry anymore. You do not need to empty the whole plate.

◇ Do not continue eating something that you do not like that much, or that you no longer hunger for, just because it's on your plate.

◇ Once you start eating, stop when you feel full or no longer interested in your food. It is better to throw away the food, than to throw it into your stomach. Eating it will not help anyone, and the money you spent will not come back into your wallet.

◇ When you feel like eating something, and you are not hungry, remember that two or three bites are enough to enjoy it. Don't eat more.

◇ If you feel hungry and expect a meal soon, don't wait. Eat something. That way you will not attack the food when it is served.

◇ You can enjoy even delicacies if you only take a small piece, enjoy the taste, and that's it. In order to feel full, it is better to eat healthy food.

◇ To truly indulge yourself is not to eat. This enjoyment lasts only a minute, and then you suffer from its results. Real indulgence is feeling good with yourself when you overcome the desire to eat, or when you do things that contribute to your body and soul like exercise or a massage.

◇ It is important to change the way you speak about food in order to separate the emotional context of eating from the physical act itself.

BE AWARE OF THE GULO

◇ Make the distinction between yourself and the Gulo! It's easier to fight the need to eat when you imagine it comes from outside.

◇ The Gulo will do anything to make you eat: it will make you feel hungry when you are full; it will nag you again and again about something until you break down and eat it; it will try to convince you to pamper yourself with food, even though it only makes you gain weight and feel bad about yourself.

◇ Recognize when the need to eat comes from the Gulo. Use the techniques described in this book to overcome it.

◇ Every victory over the Gulo weakens it a bit, and each time it triumphs over you, it gets twice as strong.

◇ The war against the Gulo is in all areas of life. Every victory or defeat affects your eating habits

◇ It is OK to lose sometimes. Everybody does. It is crucial to know how to forgive yourself. Beating yourself up will merely make the Gulo stronger and weaken you.

9 798333 017772